Explore Buffalo's Park and Cultural District

DATES IN THE STATES

A COUPLE TRAVELING THE UNITED STATES ON A BUDGET

I0459342

Mystery Date
Buffalo, NY

By Dates in the States

![Photograph of a museum with columns and a fountain in front]

SPONSOR

THIS MYSTERY DATE IS SPONSORED BY:

Hatchets & Hops

Hatchets & Hops is one of Buffalo's most unique entertainment destinations. Opened in 2016 as one of the first three axe-throwing bars in the United States, they've built a reputation as a premier spot for fun, friendly competition and unforgettable nights out.

Their guided axe-throwing competitions feature doubles matches and elimination rounds, ensuring both beginners and seasoned throwers have a blast. Beyond the bar, Hatchets & Hops also brings the excitement to your events with their mobile Axe Wagon, perfect for weddings, parties, and corporate outings.

Whether you're looking for a unique date night, a night out with friends, or a memorable group activity, Hatchets & Hops delivers energy, excitement, and a one-of-a-kind Buffalo experience.

Learn more or book your experience → hatchetsandhops.com

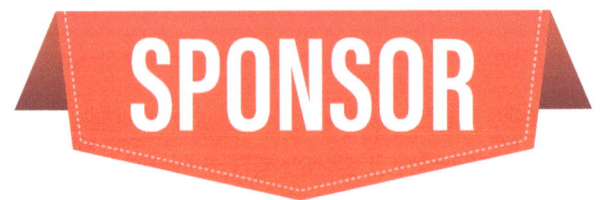

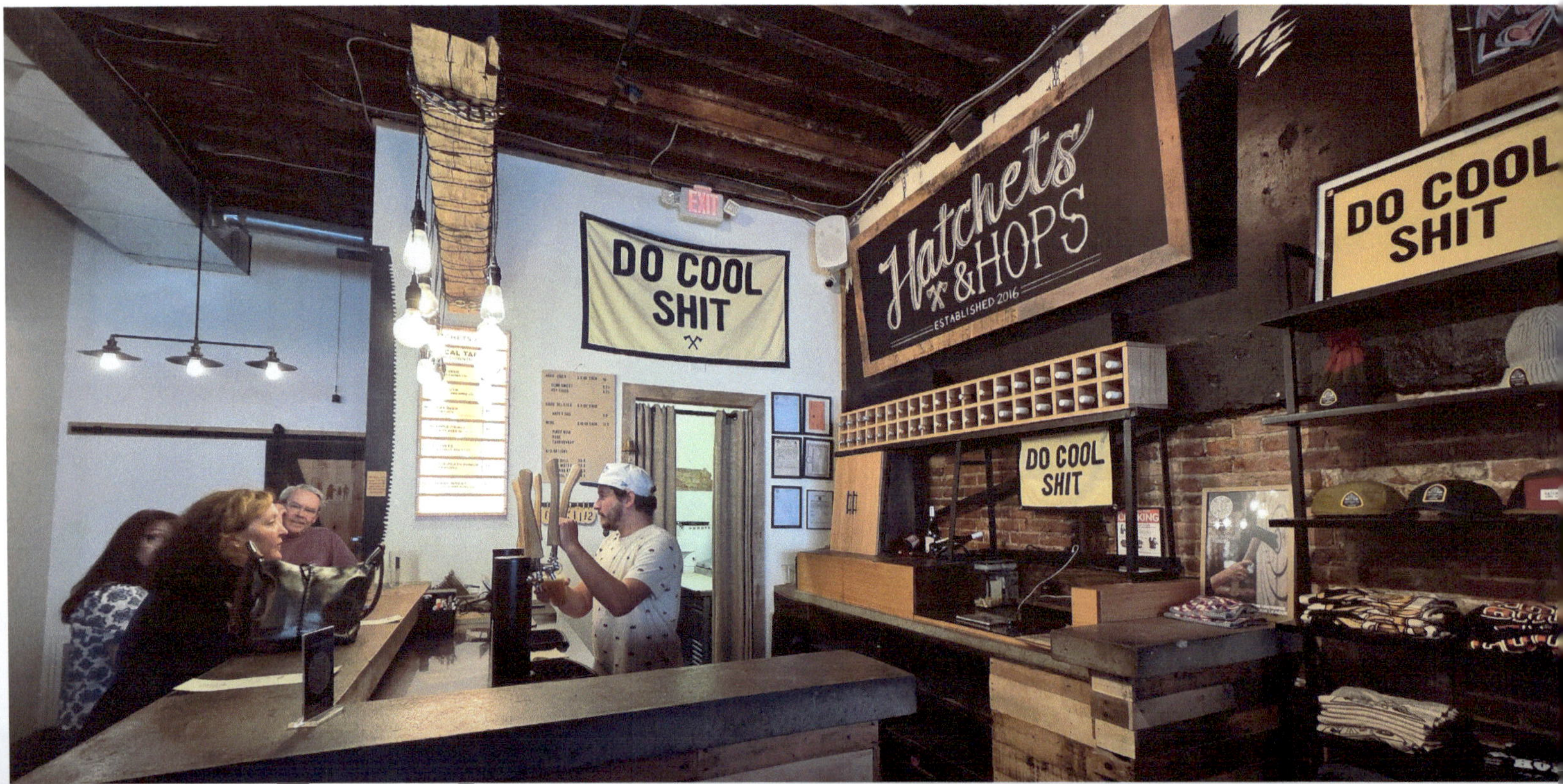

"Our passion is travel, and we want to share our adventures to inspire others to explore the world with their loved ones. Dare to live beyond the box."

Dates in the States

Introduction

Hey there! We're Crystal and Shane, the duo behind Dates in the States, where we share our love for discovering unique adventures, unforgettable moments, and hidden gems across the U.S. Whether you're searching for a fun date idea, a new place to explore, or just a little inspiration, we've got you covered!

Our Mystery Date Books are designed to help couples (and adventurous friends!) shake up their routine and experience the best local spots in a fun, intentional way. Inside, you'll find a curated collection of date ideas. Each one meant to be completed over the course of a single day in a specific neighborhood. All of which are a surprise until you flip the page!

It's like a little challenge to break out of your comfort zone, support local, and make memories that stick. We hope this book helps you laugh more, explore more, and connect more, with each other and with your city. Let the mystery begin!

Here's What To Expect:

In this Mystery Date Book, we're taking you on a playful adventure through Buffalo's park and cultural district, exploring cozy cafés, scenic parks, unique museums, and one-of-a-kind experiences.

Here's what to expect for your day ahead:

Start your morning with a relaxing coffee and breakfast to fuel your adventure. Next, soak in art and culture at a local museum, then enjoy a peaceful stroll around a scenic lake and wander along leafy park trails. Amp up the energy with a playful, competitive experience, but be sure to book ahead for your axe-throwing session, and plan your day around open hours to make the most of each stop.

This date is all about exploring Buffalo's charm, enjoying new experiences, and making memories!

1st Stop

Jam Parkside
301 Parkside Ave
Buffalo, NY 14214

Start your Buffalo adventure with a cozy breakfast stop at JAM Parkside, a charming corner café nestled near Delaware Park right across from the Buffalo Zoo. This local favorite is known for its laid-back vibe, friendly baristas, and delicious small bites.

Grab a latte or cold brew, and enjoy one of their signature breakfast sandwiches, bagels, or freshly baked pastries. Whether you sit inside the bright, airy café or people-watch from the sidewalk tables, JAM Parkside sets the perfect tone for a relaxed morning date in the city.

Second Stop

Buffalo AKG Art Museum

1285 Elmwood Ave
Buffalo, NY 14222

Next up, take in some culture at the Buffalo Art Museum. Even if you skip the ticket, the building itself is a work of art. You'll be wowed by its striking architecture, grand steps, and the iconic fountain out front.

Art lovers will want to step inside, too: the museum's galleries are filled with incredible pieces that make for a truly memorable experience. Whether you're admiring sculptures outdoors or exploring the collections inside, this stop is a memorable part of your Buffalo adventure!

Third Stop

Hoyt Lake

199 Lincoln Pkwy
Buffalo, NY 14222

Take a peaceful stroll around Hoyt Lake in Delaware Park and let the calm scenery set the tone for your day. With shimmering water, leafy paths, and serene spots to pause, it's the perfect place to slow down, enjoy the outdoors, and soak in the natural beauty of Buffalo.

If time allows, wander along the park's numerous trails and discover hidden corners of greenery. Depending on the season, you might catch a glimpse of the Rose Garden in bloom or enjoy the changing colors of the trees in fall. Whether you're chatting on a bench, snapping a few photos, or just letting the lake reflect your thoughts, Hoyt Lake is a peaceful pause in your Buffalo adventure.

Fourth Stop

The Terrace at Delaware Park

199 Lincoln Pkwy
Buffalo, NY 14222

After your stroll through the park and possibly the rose garden, you'll find a great lunch spot. So, if your stomach is ready for a break, head to The Terrace at Delaware Park for a casual bite to eat with a view. Overlooking Hoyt Lake, this charming spot serves up delicious bites while letting you soak in the scenery.

Keep in mind: lunch is only available on weekends, so if your timing doesn't line up, don't worry! There will be plenty of other opportunities to grab a bite along your Buffalo adventure, and sometimes it's nice to save room for the next stop.

Fifth Stop

Hatchets & Hops

505 Main St
Buffalo, NY 14203

Your next stop is one for the competitive spirits! Head to Hatchets & Hops, one of the area's first axe-throwing bars. **Be sure to book ahead to secure your spot.** Grab a drink at the cozy speakeasy-style bar, where seasonal beers are on tap (including a "mystery beer" because we all love a good surprise), plus ciders, wine, and non-alcoholic options.

If you didn't grab lunch earlier, fuel up with snacks like pretzels, churros, or shareable pizzas before stepping into the ring. Then, it's time to play to win! You'll start with a training session before diving in to Round Robin, then move into elimination rounds where bragging rights are on the line. Energetic, playful, and unforgettable, this stop is perfect for those looking for a unique experience in Buffalo.

Final Stop

Streetlight Brasserie

5 E Huron St

Buffalo, NY 14203

We may have included a few extra food stops in this book, but Buffalo has some amazing spots, so why not treat yourself? After your axe-throwing competition, you might be hungry and not quite ready to end the day.

Head to Streetlight Brasserie for their famous chicken and waffles, or explore other menu highlights that catch your eye. Whether you're craving something hearty, sweet, or shareable, it's the perfect way to cap off your Buffalo adventure with a tasty finale.

Add Your Photos

Thank you for joining us on this mystery date adventure! We hope you've enjoyed the delightful experiences and memorable moments we've crafted just for you in Buffalo's park and cultural district.

But the adventure doesn't stop here! Keep exploring exciting mystery dates in other cities and uncover new experiences across the U.S. by visiting our website, DatesintheStates.com. There, you can purchase both physical copies and digital downloads of our mystery date books.

Plus, don't miss out on our Mystery Date Book Club, where you can receive a brand-new mystery date book every month!
Tag us in your date photos on social media! @datesinthestates

About the Creators

Crystal, the writer and creator, is a storyteller at heart. When she's not uncovering hidden gems for the next date night idea, she runs her own digital marketing company, helping small businesses improve their content marketing, increase visibility in their communities, and streamline their online presence.
Visit: crystalstatskey.com

Shane, her husband and partner in adventure, is a dedicated personal trainer and the owner of Beekstar Fitness in Irondequoit, NY. He specializes in working with clients who have limited mobility, helping them build muscle and focus on pain areas so they can regain strength and confidence in their daily lives.
Visit: beekstarfitness.com

Crystal and Shane have explored every U.S. state except Alaska (coming soon!) and are now visiting countries in alphabetical order. Whether road-tripping or curating Mystery Date experiences, they're always chasing their next adventure.

Local Love

A few local gems in Buffalo worth exploring on your next date.

PARKSIDE MEADOW
COMFY AMERICAN TAVERN
2 RUSSELL ST, BUFFALO, NY 14214

ALICE, EVER AFTER BOOKS
ADORABLE BOOKSTORE
295 PARKSIDE AVE, BUFFALO, NY 14214

BUFFALO ZOO
LIONS, TIGERS AND BEARS, OH MY!
300 PARKSIDE AVE, BUFFALO, NY 14214

Want to see your business here? See the next page for details on how to join!

Want to be featured?

MYSTERY DATE BOOK PACKAGES

—

Are you a small business looking to reach new customers? Feature your business in our next Mystery Date Book! Choose from our partnership packages below to connect with couples seeking unique experiences and exclusive deals.

Package One
LOCAL LOVE LISTING

—

A quick shoutout to show you're part of the neighborhood vibe.

Listed in the "Local Love" section of your designated neighborhood date book

Includes business name, address, and social link

Optional: Offer a small promo (e.g., 10% off for book holders)

1 social media shout-out when the book launches

$75

Package Two
FEATURE STOP

—

You're not just a business— you're part of the experience.

Marked as a "Must-Stop" on a Mystery Date

Full-page feature in the book with your story, offerings and photo

Includes 1 social media feature — a dedicated post and story highlighting your business

Note: To ensure each feature is genuine and experience-based, we require a hosted visit prior to inclusion.

$600

Package Three
PARTNER & SELLER

—

Be the spot and the source.

Everything in Tier 2

PLUS: Option to sell the Mystery Date Books at your location

Includes a bulk purchase of 10 books (yours to price + sell)

Keep 100% of the profits from in-store sales

Bonus: Have a featured "sponsored by" page and listed as an official pickup location in our promotions

$1,000

Prices are subject to change

Feel free to reach us at any time by sending us an email to say hi and to learn more! We look forward to hearing from you.

| www.datesinthestates.com | datesinthestatesblog@gmail.com |

Sponsors & Affiliates

Our sponsors and affiliates help make our adventures possible! Explore the amazing brands and businesses that support our community.

Wanderful

Wanderful is a global community for women who love to travel. Connect, explore, and join a local hub near you!

Join our Book Club!

Join our Mystery Date Book Club and be part of a travel-inspired community, discovering unique local adventures together!

HomeExchange

HomeExchange lets you swap homes with travelers worldwide for authentic, affordable stays. Join today and travel differently!

Shop our books at a store near you!

Little Button Craft
658 South Ave.
Rochester, NY 14620

The Pawsitive Cat Cafe
120 East Ave. Ste 100
Rochester, NY 14604

Yesterday's Muse Books
32 West Main St.
Webster, NY 14580

Nashville Souvenirs
2613 McGavock Pk,
Nashville, TN 37214

Music Valley Antiques
2416 Music Valley Dr.
Nashville, TN 37214

Barnes & Noble
1 Walden Galleria g113,
Buffalo, NY 14225

Abundance Food Co-op
571 South Ave,
Rochester, NY 14620

Union Tavern
4565 Culver Rd,
Irondequoit, NY 14622

DATES IN THE STATES

A COUPLE TRAVELING THE UNITED
STATES ON A BUDGET

🌐

datesinthestates.com

✉

datesinthestatesblog@gmail.com

📍

Based in Rochester, NY

CONNECT WITH US ON SOCIAL!
@DATESINTHESTATES